THAT'S FOR SHORE

Riddles from the Beach

by June Swanson
pictures by Susan Slattery Burke

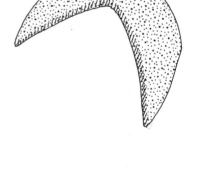

Lerner Publications Company · Minneapolis

To John, for letting me take advantage of his sense of humor —J.S.

To my wonderful daughter, Shea, for her incredible inspiration in this first year of her life —S.S.B.

Copyright © 1991 by Lerner Publications Company

Library of Congress Cataloging-in-Publication Data

Swanson, June.
   That's for shore : riddles from the beach / by June Swanson;
pictures by Susan Slattery Burke.

      p.   cm.–(You must be joking!)
   Summary: Presents riddles about the beach, such as "What do you
call a beach party? A shell-abration."
   ISBN 0-8225-2332-9
   1. Riddles, Juvenile. 2. Beaches–Juvenile humor. 3. Ocean–
Juvenile humor. [1. Beaches–Wit and humor. 2. Seashore–Wit and
humor. 3. Marine animals–Wit and humor. 4. Riddles.] I. Burke, Susan
Slattery, ill. II. Title. III. Series.
PN6371.5.S88   1991   818'.5402–dc20   90-48961
                                                          CIP
Manufactured in the United States of America   AC

1 2 3 4 5 6 7 8 9 10 00 99 98 97 96 95 94 93 92 91

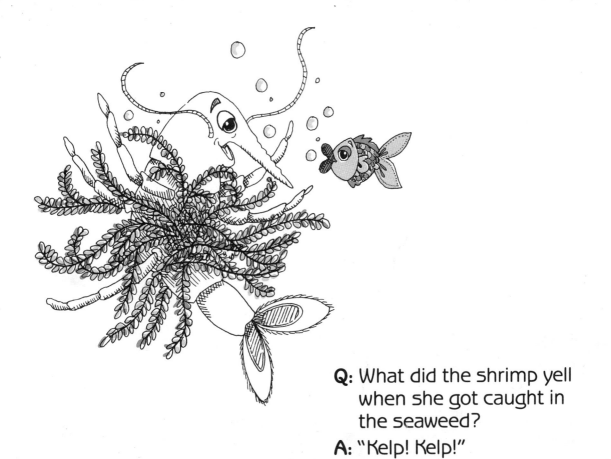

Q: What did the shrimp yell when she got caught in the seaweed?

A: "Kelp! Kelp!"

Q: Why did all the fish pick up the little lobster?
A: They thought he was just a shrimp.

Q: What did one whale shout to the other whale one foggy day?

A: "You're out of sight!"

Q: Why are mountains like ocean waves?

A: They both have white caps.

Q: What do you get when you cross a flamingo with a salmon?

A: A pink bird that flies upstream.

Q: What do you get when you cross an ocean with a hermit crab?

A: Wet.

Q: What do you call a lobster after it's one year old?
A: Two years old.

Q: How did the mother crab take her baby to the beach?
A: In a dune buggy.

Q: What do you call a baby squid?
A: A squid kid.

Q: What do you call the baby squid's hat?
A: A squid kid lid.

Q: What happened when the baby squid played hide-and-seek?
A: The squid kid hid.

Q: What did the whale call the sandy hills on the beach?
A: I dune know. What?

Q: What's pink, has long legs, and calls "B-11, I-25, and G-52?"

A: A flabingo.

Q: What goes tick-tock-grit, tick-tock-grit?

A: The sands of time.

Q: Why did the whale rush to scratch his back on the reef?

A: Because he knew an itch in time saves nine.

Q: How can you tell when the ocean's friendly?

A: The tidal wave.

Q: What fish is good at selling used cars?
A: A sailfish.

Q: What did the farmer raise in the sand?
A: A beach umbrella.

Q: What did the codfish drive to the beach?
A: Her Codillac.

Q: Why won't the lobster ever run out of money?
A: He lives in a bank full of sand dollars.

Q: How did the police drive to the beach?
A: In a squid car.

Q: What would you call a jail full of seagulls?
A: Birds of a feather locked together.

Q: How did one clam call the other clam?

A: On his shell-ular phone.

Q: Why couldn't the waves reach the shore?
A: They were tide up.

Q: Where do you read the beach news?
A: In the sandpaper.

Q: What did the octopus use to paint pictures?

A: An eel-sel.

Q: What color is a catfish?

A: Purr-ple.

Q: What's grey and orange and purple and blue and yellow and red and green?

A: A whale wearing surfing shorts.

Q: Why couldn't the whale hear the ocean roar?

A: Because she was hard of herring.

Q: What would you call a chorus line of a thousand fish?
A: A grand fin-ale.

Q: Who plays for the beach parades?
A: The bass band.

Q: What did the fish roll out for King Crab?

A: The red carp-et.

Q: Where does King Crab live?

A: In a sand castle.

Q: Who cleans King Crab's sand castle?

A: The mermaids.

Q: What would you call an octopus that squirts disappearing ink?

A: Invisible.

Q: Why did the black cat-fish go to the beach on Halloween?

A: She was looking for a sand-witch.

Q: Why is a seagull on the beach like the North Pole?

A: They both have sandy claws.

Q: How did the lobster decorate for the holidays?

A: With a Christmas reef.

Q: Why did the pelican refuse to pay for his meal?

A: His bill was too big.

Q: Why was the shark following the fishing boat?

A: She was looking for a hand-out.

Q: Why wasn't the shark sorry when he bit the large fish?

A: He did it on porpoise.

Q: How do you make a brown pelican float?

A: With a scoop of ice cream, a can of root beer, and a pelican.

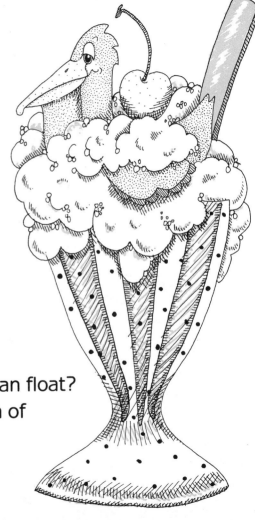

Q: Where do sea turtles live?
A: In shell-ters.

Q: Why wasn't the crab hurt when the house fell on him?

A: It was a lighthouse.

Q: What kind of bear lives in the ocean?

A: A bear-acuda.

Q: Why couldn't the shell move?

A: She was conched out.

Q: How do you get to the ocean?

A: Go left at the tern on the beach.

Q: How did the ocean announcer end her program?

A: "Tuna tomorrow for the next exciting chapter."

Q: How do you begin a fairy tale about a jelly fish?

A: "Once upon a slime…"

Q: Where do seahorses live?

A: In barn-acles.

Q: What did Moby-Dick put by his front door?

A: A whale-come mat.

Q: How often did Jonah go to the beach?

A: Just once in a whale.

Q: What did Cinderella lose at the beach?

A: A glass flipper.

Q: Why didn't the shark bite Donald?

A: Donald ducked.

Q: How did the whale describe his new rowboat?

A: "Totally oarsome!"

Q: Why did the crab go to the beach?

A: To see the ocean wave.

Q: What do you call the ocean's comings and goings?

A: Current events.

Q: Why did the whale give up surfing?

A: She was board with it.

Q: Why was the clam coloring eggs?
A: To help the oyster bunny.

Q: Why did the pelican send flowers to the seagull?
A: She was his gull friend.

Q: What is the border between two oceans called?
A: A sea lion.

Q: Why did the fish wear a black cap and gown?
A: He was graduating from his school.

Q: What did the little shark have in her lunch box?
A: Peanut butter and jellyfish sandwiches.

Q: What position did the fish play in the beach baseball game?

A: First bass.

Q: Why didn't the surfer believe the shark's story?

A: There was something fishy about it.

Q: Why couldn't the sailors play cards on their boat?

A: The captain was sitting on the deck.

Q: What do you have when surfers raise their hands?

A: Swaying palms.

Q: What toy did the shark take to the beach?

A: His finner tube.

Q: How did the sun heat the ocean?

A: One ray at a time.

Q: What do you call a beach party?

A: A shell-ebration.

Q: Who wears a red, white, and blue swim suit?

A: Uncle Sand.

ABOUT THE AUTHOR

June Swanson began her career by writing magazine articles and short stories—both for children and adults. After having almost 200 published, she turned to writing books. This is her fourth published book. June is a graduate of the University of Texas and Florida Atlantic University and has been both an elementary school teacher and the teacher of college writing courses. She has four children and, at last count, seven grandchildren. She lives by the beach.

ABOUT THE ARTIST

Susan Slattery Burke loves to illustrate fun-loving characters, especially animals. To her, each of them has a personality all its own. Her satisfaction comes when the characters come to life for the reader as well. Susan lives in Minneapolis, Minnesota, with her husband, her daughter, and their dog and cat. A graduate of the University of Minnesota, Susan enjoys sculpting, travel, illustrating, chasing her daughter, and being outdoors.

You Must Be Joking

Alphabatty: Riddles from A to Z
Help Wanted: Riddles about Jobs
Here's to Ewe: Riddles about Sheep
Hide and Shriek: Riddles about Ghosts and Goblins
Ho Ho Ho! Riddles about Santa Claus
I Toad You So: Riddles about Frogs and Toads
On with the Show: Show Me Riddles
Out on a Limb: Riddles about Trees and Plants
That's for Shore: Riddles from the Beach
Weather or Not: Riddles for Rain and Shine
What's Gnu? Riddles from the Zoo
Wing It! Riddles about Birds